ZiGGY FACES LiFE

by Tom Wilson

A SIGNET BOOK

NEW AMERICAN LIBRARY

TIMES MIRROR

Published by arrangement with Andrews and McMeel, Inc.,
a Universal Press Syndicate Company

ZIGGY FACES LIFE was originally published by
Andrews & McMeel, Inc., as a 128-page large-format paperback.
The Signet edition ZIGGY FACES LIFE comprises the first
half of the book, and ZIGGY FACES LIFE . . . AGAIN!
the second half.

Ⓞ

SIGNET TRADEMARK REG. U.S. PAT. OFF. AND FOREIGN COUNTRIES
REGISTERED TRADEMARK—MARCA REGISTRADA
HECHO EN CHICAGO, U.S.A.

SIGNET, SIGNET CLASSICS, MENTOR, PLUME, MERIDIAN AND NAL
BOOKS are published by The New American Library, Inc.,
1633 Broadway, New York, New York 10019

First Signet Printing, March, 1982

4   5   6   7   8   9   10   11   12   13

PRINTED IN THE UNITED STATES OF AMERICA

19

23

24

27

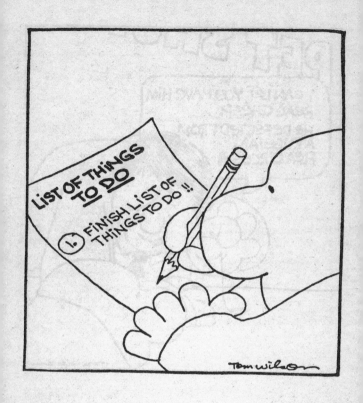

34

43

45

47

48

51

52

54

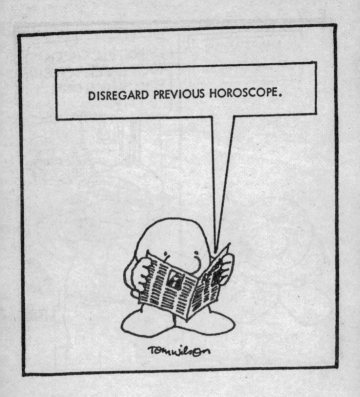

75

93

99

100

111

113

120

121

123